NOSE is not TOES

Glenn Doman
Illustrated by Janet Doman

The Better Baby Press

TO KATIE

who has taught more babies than anybody

Published by The Better Baby Press,
an institute of the Institutes for the Achievement of Human Potential
8801 Stenton Avenue,
Philadelphia, PA 19118 U.S.A.
Manufactured in the United States of America

Design: PUBLICATION SERVICES

          Third edition, first printing
          Second edition, three printings
          First edition, four printings

Library of Congress Cataloging in Publication Data
Doman, Glenn J.
Doman, Janet J.

          Nose is not toes

          1. Infants 2. Education, pre-school I. Title

ISBN: 0-944349-62-5

NOSE is not TOES

Glenn Doman

Everyone knows

that nose is not toes,

but nose **sounds** like toes.

That <u>is</u> a funny one!

Because nose is at one

end of you,

on your face,

nose

J.J.D.

and toes are at the
other

end of you,

on

your foot.

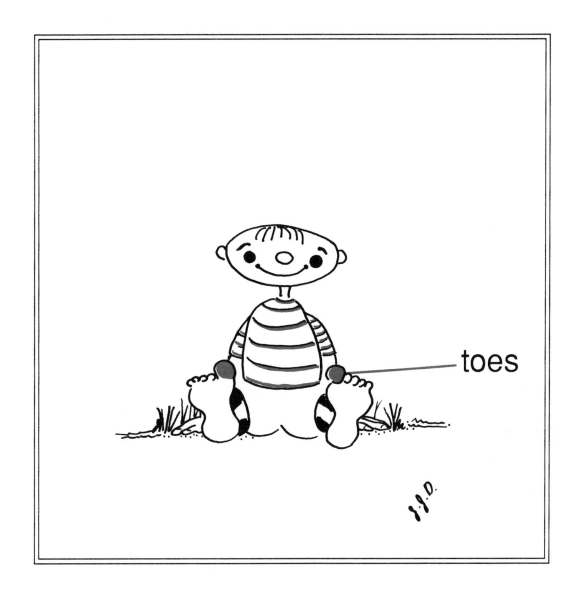

toes

Everyone knows

that nose is not toes.

But nose looks like
toes

a little bit.

Because they both have

this ——— O

and this —————— S

and this ——— E

in them

somewhere,

but mixed up

a little bit.

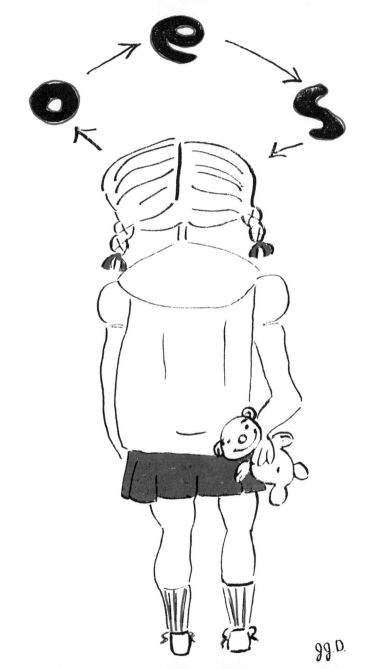

Everyone knows

that nose is not toes.

Most of all

a porpoise knows

because

a porpoise has

a nose

but

no toes

at all.

Everyone knows

that mouth is not hair.

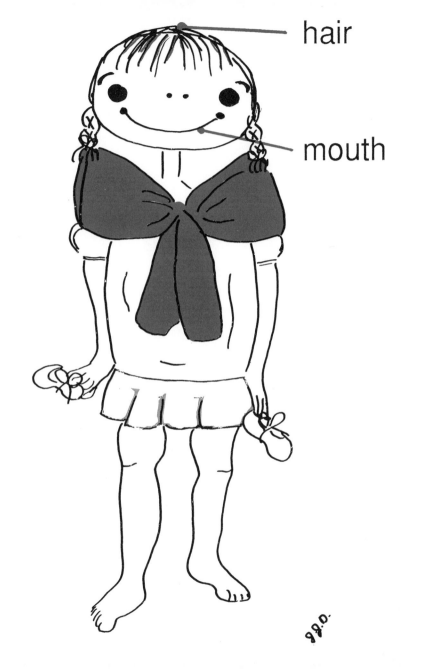

hair

mouth

How could it be!

I know you see ——

that it could not be.

Mouth is <u>not</u> hair!

Everyone knows

that head is not elbow.

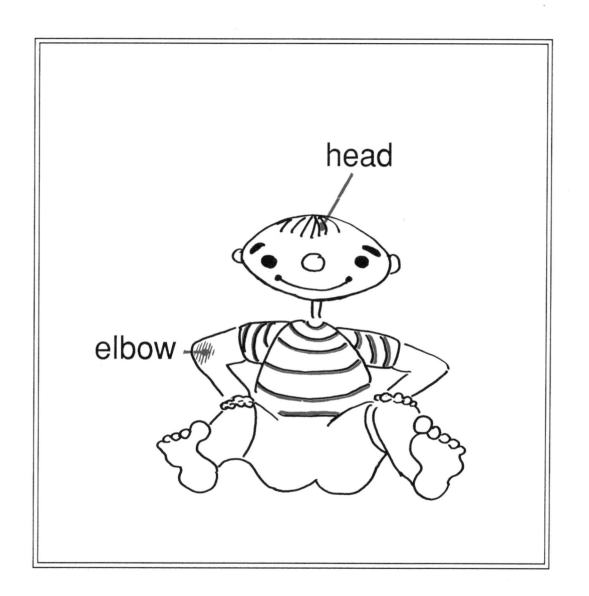

Everyone knows

81

that tongue is not
arm.

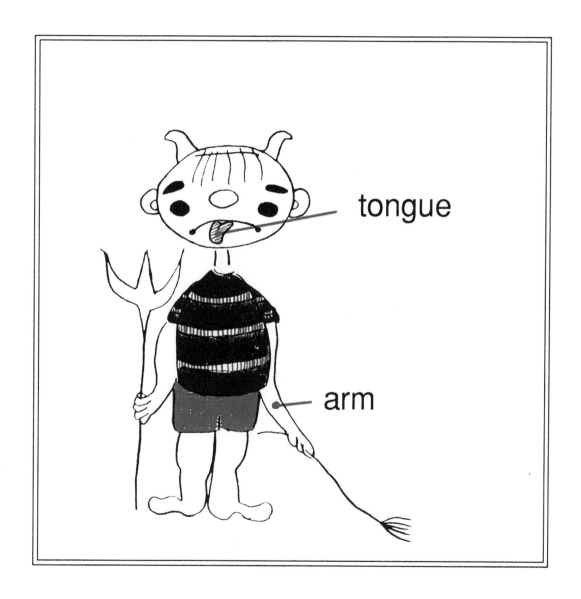

tongue

arm

85

How could it be!

I know you see ——

that it could not be.

Tongue is <u>not</u> arm!

Everyone knows

that teeth is not leg.

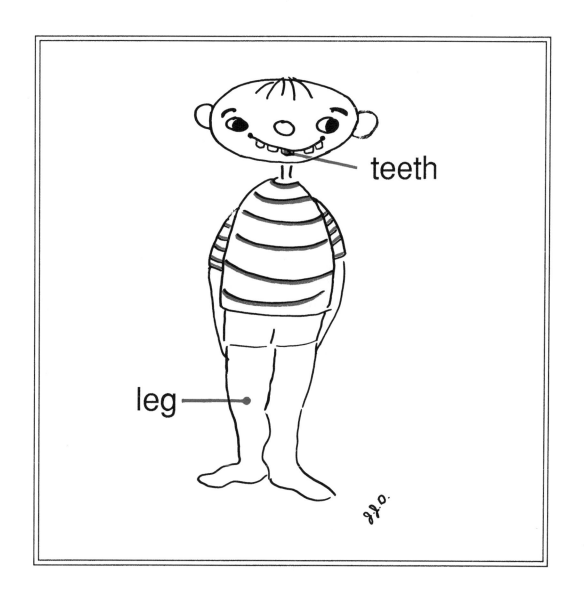

teeth

leg

Everyone knows

that neck is not hand.

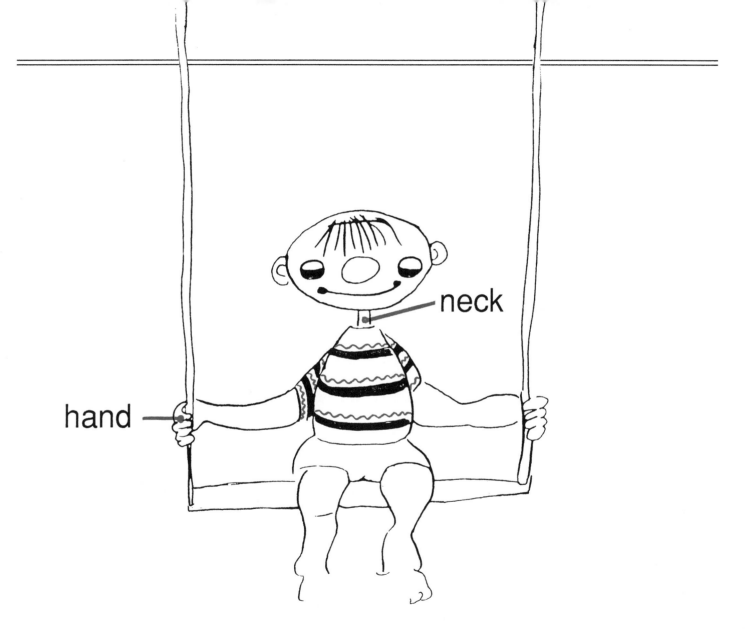

neck

hand

Most of all

a porpoise knows

because . . .

a porpoise has

a mouth

and a head

and a tongue

and a neck

and teeth

but no

elbow,

arm,

leg,

hair

or hand

at all.

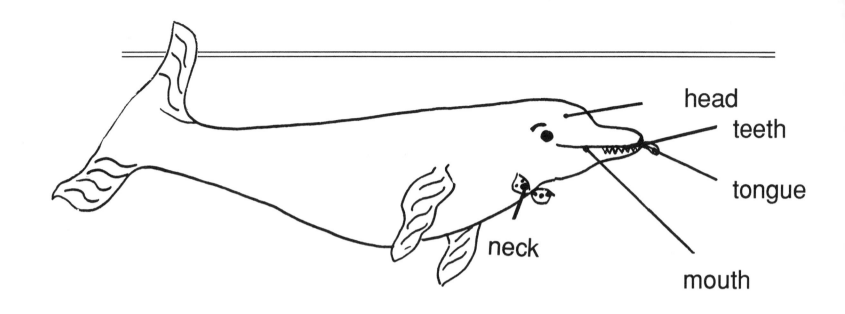

head

teeth

tongue

neck

mouth

But no elbow, arm, leg, hair or hand at all.

Only people

have a cheek

cheek

129

except, —— maybe

my dog, Tiki.

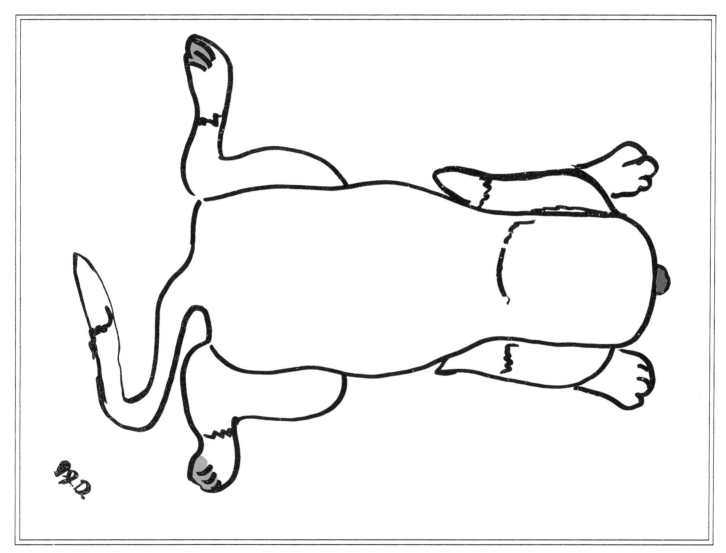

Mother says

he has lots of cheek

and thinks he is

a people.

About the book

In 1964 the publication of the book *How To Teach Your Baby To Read* by Glenn Doman signaled the beginning of a revolution in the way children's books are written and designed. *NOSE is not TOES* was the first book designed to be read by two- and three-year-old children. Written by Glenn Doman and illustrated by his fourteen-year-old daughter, Janet, the story behind this book is really the story of the Institutes for the Achievement of Human Potential in Philadelphia.

The pioneering work of the Institutes was begun by its founder, Glenn Doman, prior to World War II. In 1945 Glenn resumed his work with brain-injured children, which led to discoveries in child brain development that proved vital to well children, especially in the area of early reading.

Reading programs were designed and taught to mothers of severely brain-injured children by the Institutes under the direction of Katie Doman, Glenn's wife. By the time *How To Teach Your Baby To Read* was published, it was common for two- and three-year-old brain-injured children to be able to read, and mothers of well children were discovering that their children could read too. To this day mothers come to the Institutes from around the world to learn the principles of child brain development and to gain the practical knowledge of how to use those principles to design their own home programs.

The Institutes' staff continue to search for and develop new programs and materials and to teach parents of well and brain-injured children. Each year the staff sees thousands of parents and children in Philadelphia and at locations around the world.

NOSE is not TOES was the first step toward making available to mothers the hundreds of children's books written by the Institutes' staff and friends. It is intended to be used and enjoyed as part of the reading program outlined in Glenn Doman's books, *How to Teach Your Baby To Read* and *How To Multiply Your Baby's Intelligence*.

About the author

Glenn Doman graduated from the University of Pennsylvania in 1940 and began pioneering the field of child brain development. This work was interrupted by distinguished service as a combat infantry officer in World War II. He founded the Institutes for the Achievement of Human Potential in 1955.

By the early 1960s Glenn's work with brain-injured children led to vital discoveries about the growth and development of well children. In 1963 he wrote *How To Teach Your Baby To Read*, the classic book that has been translated into twenty languages and read by millions of mothers the world over.

His proudest possession is the more than 100,000 letters from mothers around the world telling him of the joy they experienced in teaching their babies to read.

Among honors from many nations he was knighted by the Brazilian government for his outstanding work on behalf of the children of the world.

About the illustrator

Janet Doman grew up at the Institutes and was pitching in to help brain-injured children by the time she was nine years old. She was directly involved in the Institutes' groundbreaking work in early reading.

At fourteen she illustrated *NOSE is not TOES* after her father asked her to draw some pictures of kids that could then be turned over to a "real" illustrator.

The illustrators who were tried changed the original sketches into slick, unbelievable scenes.

After the author told several illustrators, "It has to be more like the originals," he finally decided that what was needed *was* the originals.

Today Janet is Director of the Institutes for the Achievement of Human Potential.

More information about how to teach your child

Books:
How To Teach Your Baby To Read
What To Do About Your Brain-Injured
Child
How To Multiply Your Baby's
Intelligence
How To Give Your Baby Encyclopedic
Knowledge
How To Teach Your Baby Math
How To Teach Your Baby To Be
Physically Superb

Children's Books:
The Life & Times of Inigo McKenzie
Series
NOSE is not TOES

The Gentle Revolution Series Videos:
How To Teach Your Baby To Read
How To Give Your Baby Encyclopedic
Knowledge
How To Teach Your Baby Math

Materials:
How To Teach Your Baby To Read Kit
How To Teach Your Baby Math Kit

Courses:
How To Multiply Your Baby's
Intelligence Course
What To Do About Your Brain-Injured
Child Course

How To Teach Your Baby Catalogs:
The Better Baby Catalog
The Programs of the Institutes

For more information call or write:
The Institutes for the Achievement of
Human Potential
8801 Stenton Avenue
Philadelphia, PA 19118 USA

Phone: 1-800-344-MOTHER
           1-215-233-2050
FAX: 1-215-233-3940

This book contains the following single words:

a
all
and
are
arm
at

be
because
bit
both
but

cheek
could

dog

elbow
end
everyone
except

face
foot
funny

hair
hand
has
have
he
head
how

I
in
is
it

know
knows

leg
like
little
looks
lots

maybe
mixed
most
mother
mouth
my

neck
no
nose
not

of
on
one
only
or
other

people
porpoise

says
see
sounds
somewhere

teeth
that
the
them
they
thinks
this
Tiki
toes
tongue

up

you
your